ALFRED'S SACRED PERFORMER COLLECTIONS

LATE INTERMEDIATE TO EARLY ADVANCED PIANO

10 Arrangements of Contemporary Christian Favorites

Arranged by **MELODY BOBER**

All the earth bows down to you;
they sing praise to you,
they sing praise to your name.
—Psalm 66:4 (NIV®)

In my life, the act of praise is a daily offering. It gives glory and honor to our Creator, Redeemer, and Friend, and opens up a deeper union with Him. But most important, it allows me to focus on God rather than myself. The word *praise* is found in the Bible over 200 times, and throughout the ages numerous songs have been written with praise as the central theme.

This collection features contemporary songwriters who praise God for His greatness ("How Great Is Our God"), His holiness ("God of Wonders"), His mercy and love ("Amazing Grace (My Chains Are Gone)"), and His redemption ("In Christ Alone"). I hope these selections will bring a measure of hope to your heart and that students, teachers, and church musicians will enjoy performing these uplifting tunes, which all express the words of Psalm 150:6: "Let everything that has breath praise the Lord. Praise the Lord." (NIV®)

Melody Bober

Amazing Grace (My Chains Are Gone)	2
Come, Now Is the Time to Worship	12
God of Wonders	7
Here I Am to Worship	16
How Great Is Our God	20
I Will Be Here	28
In Christ Alone	32
Open the Eyes of My Heart	25
You Are My King (Amazing Love)	36
You Deliver Me	40

Produced by
Alfred Music
P.O. Box 10003
Van Nuys, CA 91410-0003
alfred.com

No part of this book shall be reproduced, arranged, adapted, recorded, publicly performed, stored in a retrieval system, or transmitted by any means without written permission from the publisher. In order to comply with copyright laws, please apply for such written permission and/or license by contacting the publisher at alfred.com/permissions.

ISBN-10: 0-7390-9519-6
ISBN-13: 978-0-7390-9519-5

Cover Photos
Close up on scriptures: © stock.xchng.com / mrnemelka • Poppy flowers in the sky: © shutterstock.com / Andrey tiyk •
Sunset on Lake Starnberger: © stock.xchng.com / Krappweis

Amazing Grace (My Chains Are Gone)

Words and Music by
Chris Tomlin and Louie Giglio
Arr. Melody Bober

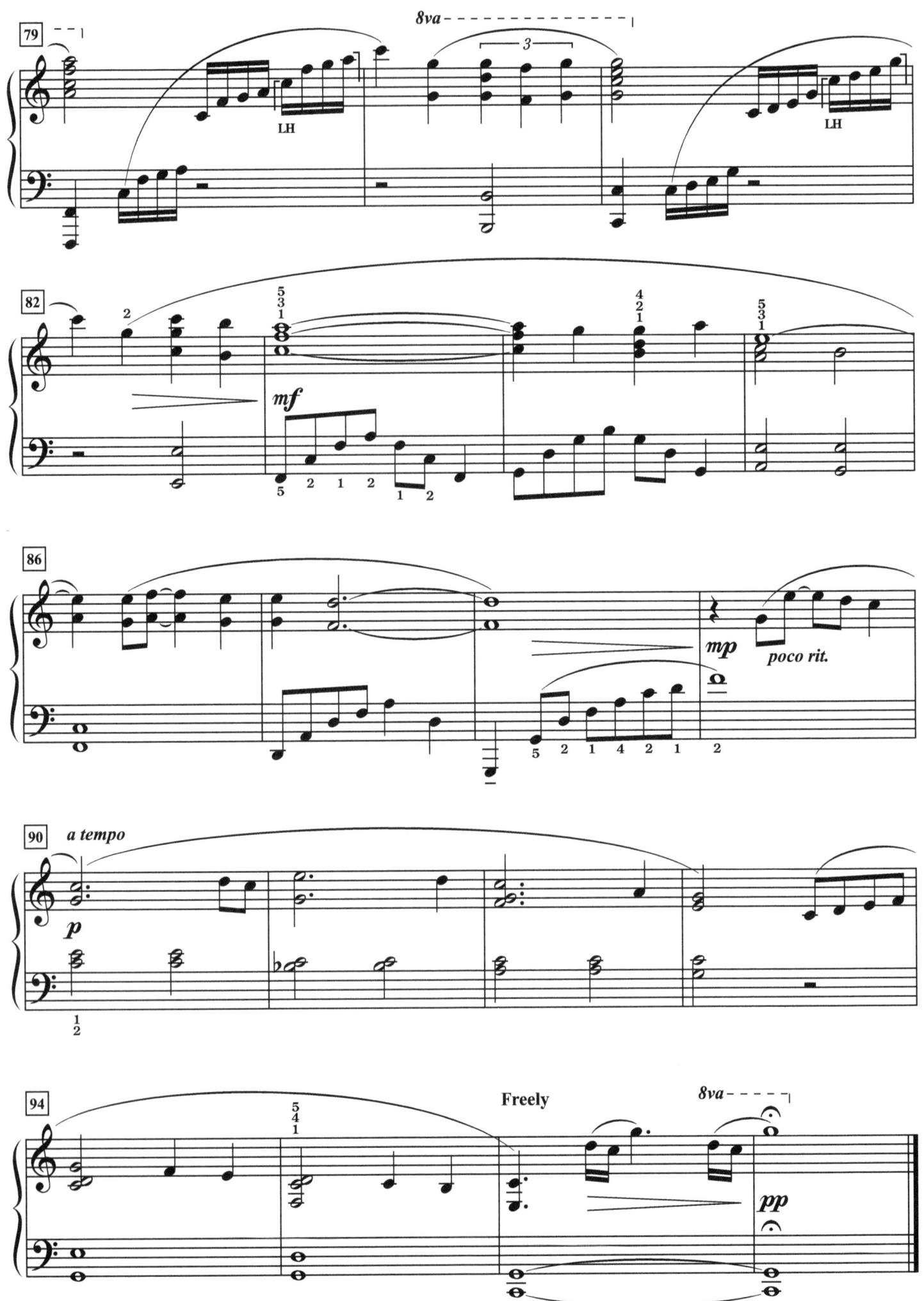

(Approx. Performance Time – 3:00)

God of Wonders

Words and Music by
Marc Byrd and Steve Hindalong
Arr. Melody Bober

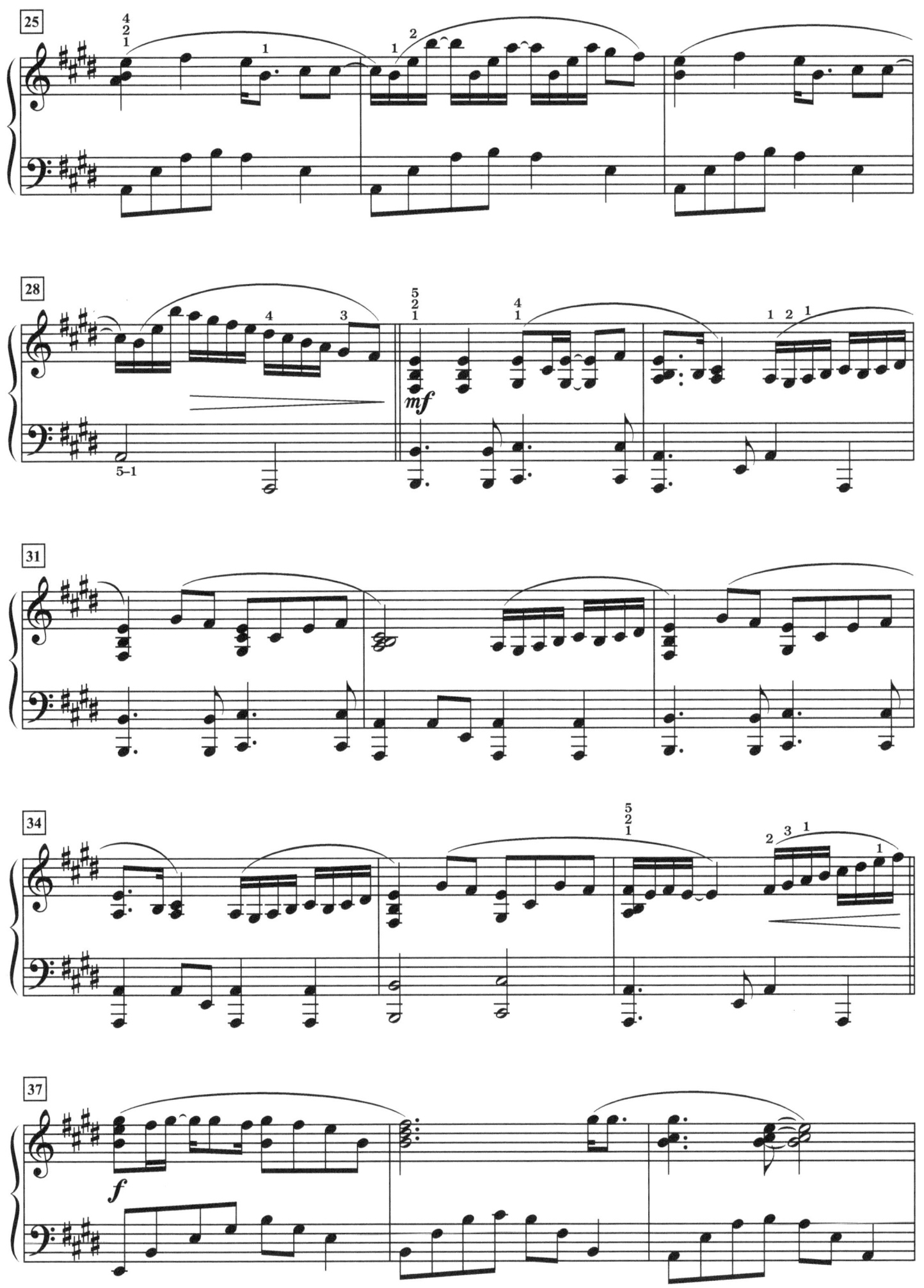

12 (Approx. Performance Time – 2:00)

Come, Now Is the Time to Worship

Words and Music by Brian Doerksen
Arr. Melody Bober

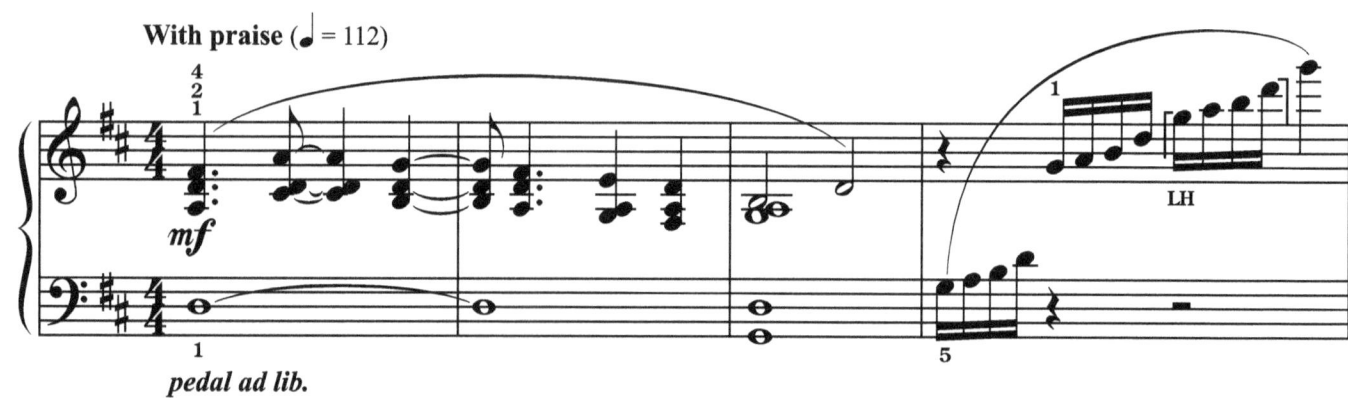

© 1998 VINEYARD SONGS (UK/EIRE) (PRS)
Administered in North America by MUSIC SERVICES, INC.
All Rights Reserved   Used by Permission

(Approx. Performance Time – 2:30)

Here I Am to Worship

Words and Music by Tim Hughes
Arr. Melody Bober

© 2001 THANKYOU MUSIC (PRS) (Administered worldwide at EMICMGPublishing.com
excluding Europe which is administered by kingswaysongs.com)
All Rights Reserved   Used by Permission

How Great Is Our God

(Approx. Performance Time – 2:30)

Words and Music by
Jesse Reeves, Chris Tomlin and Ed Cash
Arr. Melody Bober

© 2004 WORSHIPTOGETHER.COM SONGS, SIXSTEPS MUSIC and ALLETROP MUSIC (BMI)
All Rights for WORSHIPTOGETHER.COM SONGS and SIXSTEPS MUSIC Administered at EMICMGPublishing.com
All Rights for ALLETROP MUSIC Administered by MUSIC SERVICES, INC.
All Rights Reserved   Used by Permission

(Approx. Performance Time – 2:00)

Open the Eyes of My Heart

Words and Music by Paul Baloche
Arr. Melody Bober

© 1997 INTEGRITY'S HOSANNA! MUSIC
All Rights Administered at EMICMGPublishing.com
All Rights Reserved   Used by Permission

28

(Approx. Performance Time – 2:45)

I Will Be Here

Words and Music by Stephen Curtis Chapman
Arr. Melody Bober

© 1989 SPARROW SONG, GREG NELSON MUSIC and UNIVERSAL MUSIC-CAREERS
All Rights for SPARROW SONG and GREG NELSON MUSIC Administered at EMICMGPublishing.com
All Rights Reserved   Used by Permission

In Christ Alone

Words and Music by Stuart Townend and Keith Getty
Arr. Melody Bober

You Are My King (Amazing Love)

(Approx. Performance Time – 2:30)

Words and Music by Billy James Foote
Arr. Melody Bober

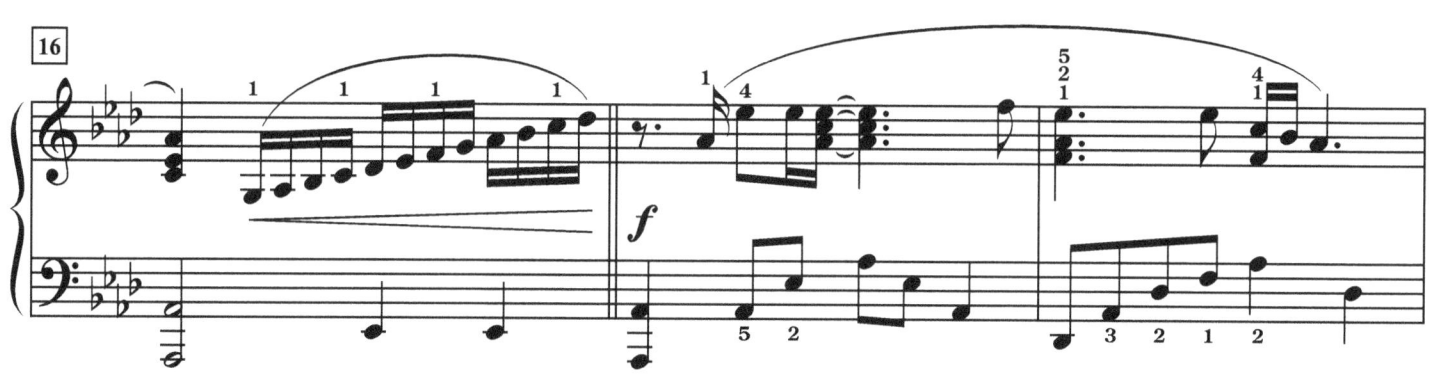

You Deliver Me

(Approx. Performance Time – 3:00)

Words and Music by
Brian Nash, Michael Post and David Pearson
Arr. Melody Bober

© 2001 CHRYSALIS ONE MUSIC PUBLISHING GROUP IRELAND LTD. (IMRO), BRIAN NASH MUSIC (ASCAP),
J-BIRD MUSIC, DAVID PEARSON MUSIC, NAKED AS A J-BIRD MUSIC and FLYING J-BIRD MUSIC
All Rights for CHRYSALIS ONE MUSIC PUBLISHING GROUP IRELAND LTD. (IMRO) and BRIAN NASH MUSIC (ASCAP)
Administered by CHRYSALIS ONE MUSIC (ASCAP)/BMG RIGHTS MANAGEMENT (US) LLC
All Rights Reserved